DON'T PLAY!!!
PRAY!!!!

The Professional Women's Guide to Identifying His Brokenness

Ina Johnson Myers

https://www.WhenSheRise.com

Disclaimer

All erudition contained in this book is given for informational and educational purposes only. The author is not a mental health care professional and the views and opinions expressed in this book are those of the authors journey and research. The author is not in any way accountable for any results or outcomes that emanate from using this material. Constructive attempts have been made to provide information that is both accurate and effective, but the author is not bound for the accuracy or use/misuse of this information.

TABLE OF CONTENTS

ACKNOWLEDGMENTS

ALL THE PRESSURES OF LIFE
WILL EITHER MAKE DIAMONDS OR DUST!!!!

I always knew God created me for a life greater than what I was living, but I had no idea what it was. I did not realize that God had already chosen me. He was just waiting for me to seek Him with all my heart.

Above all, I give thanks to my Lord and Savior, Jesus Christ. Never in my wildest dreams did I think I would ever write a book. I was compelled to write this book because there are a lot of professional women out there who are either seeking to be in a relationship or currently in a relationship who are in need of me sharing this knowledge that I have gained. Without a test, there could be no testimony. I used to have a hard time relating to people's testimonies in church because

I never struggled with any addictions or vices. I forgave pretty easily, so I did not struggle with holding grudges. I was raised by two great parents that gave me unconditional love, so I did not struggle with the issues of fatherlessness or poverty. So, despite twenty-four years of military service, raising three kids, and deploying to multiple wars, I often felt like I did not have much of a struggle to share. Be careful what you ask for because my God is truly a provider. I just praise God that struggles don't last always.

Lord, I thank you for…
My Protection/ My Direction/ My Correction

Next, I want to thank the best kids ever. I honestly used to thank God when they were younger for low-maintenance kids.

Adrian, my Lady and eldest of the bunch. My Rock when I had to work or deploy. As my lil Lady, I know you grew up with a lot on your shoulders, refereeing the other two and keeping things together while I was away. I deeply appreciated you then because I would not have been able to accomplish the things I did without the support, and I truly appreciate the woman you are now with your own family. Your strength and your loving heart show in your kids. I love you to the moon and back a few times.

Ivory, my BabyGirl and most stubborn (you got it from me honestly, but I did not mean to pass that on) of the bunch. My Second Rock in charge. I truly appreciate all you did throughout this journey, keeping all the balls in the air and kicking any under the couch that may have hit the ground after you diverted my attention elsewhere. My skydiving buddy. I appreciate the woman and businesswoman you are. I love you to the moon and back a few times.

Earnest III, my Sonshine, and baby of the bunch. I have to thank you for all the laughter that was around here. I know you often felt out-estrogened with three females in the house, but you survived it by harassing your sisters so they would either chase you or throw something at you, which would start another round of laughing as Ivory chased you up and down the stairs. I truly appreciate the man you are, and I love you to the moon and back a few times.

To my sisters Geri, Phyllis, Kathy, Brenda, Cynthia and Vickie. You have loved me and supported me throughout my entire life. I could not begin to express the depth of my gratitude and deepest appreciation for all you have done. There would not have been a military career without your support and opening your homes and your hearts to my children during school breaks, summers, and deployments. I am so proud to be one of those "Johnson Girls," and I'm looking forward to continued family trips. I deeply love and appreciate each and every one of you.

And last but by no means least…

Dad and Mom, I love you with every fiber of my being, and I miss you both so very much. I know you are in Heaven laughing and cracking jokes with each other, or Momma is telling one of her military stories as she marches around Heaven or doing some sort of community service somewhere. Dad, you never got a chance to see me fly, but I am happy you got a chance to spend time with your granddaughter, Adrian. Dad and Mom, I thank you for the moral and family values you taught us. I thank you for the love you two shared and gave to your daughters. I thank you for introducing me to a Man named Jesus. Dad, I thank you for showing me the character of a husband, you always operated with love and integrity, and I appreciate that example. Continue to Rest.

INTRODUCTION

Having come from a military family, I was exposed to the military mindset at a young age.

Both of my parents who were WWII Veterans, and my oldest sister served our great country. My mother was a 4'11 powerhouse military woman, she was a WAC and very proud of her tours of military service. She, too, was about breaking barriers. In the 1940's, not many women volunteered to serve our country because society told them that wasn't a woman's place. That box society put those women in was not strong enough to contain the determination my mother had to serve her country. Going against her family's objections, as well as those of my father's family, she enlisted. She later discovered that because she had taken some college courses, she would outrank my father which, I believe, made her enlistment that much sweeter.

So, growing up in a family of service, there was really no surprise when I joined the military myself. My military career stretched over 24 years, and as a Combat Veteran, I retired in 2006, having honorably served our country in multiple international Conflicts. Throughout my military career, I either traveled to or lived on five of the seven continents. Before my retirement, I was offered the opportunity to work overseas as a contractor, so I decided to go. I enjoyed all the opportunities and growth working overseas afforded my family and me. As an IT Professional (Network Transport, Network Administrator, Ethical Hacker and Computer Hacking Forensic Investigator) I was able to grow in my IT career field with a wealth of knowledge, applications, and experience.

Now I have dedicated my life to helping other professional women push past their struggles of emotional or mental burdens that impede their growth and hinder them from becoming the powerful laser-focused businesswomen they were fearfully and wonderfully designed to be.

CHAPTER 1

THE MAKING

My beginnings started in Gary, Indiana, being raised in a two-parent home with six sisters. The love and laughter that filled our home were always in excess. Both my father and mother were WWII Veterans, and they ensured that solid Christian principles were instilled in us. Our family is quite big, so we had lots of cousins, aunts, uncles, and grandparents. As I got older, I truly appreciated being raised by parents who really loved each other and also loved their children. When I was young, I took that for granted, but growing up, I found that my reality was more of a fantasy for many people. As I think back on their interactions, I realize that they actually loved being with each other; there was hardly ever a dull moment when they were with each other. I can still picture my mom throwing her head back and laughing hard during their little conversations. One vital component of marriage is truly liking the person you are married to, and this was something that I did not understand until I got married myself. I assumed that if you deeply loved someone, despite any of the red flags, you obviously liked them, but life has proven that to be not actually the case.

I grew up with people always around; we spent most of our summers hanging out with neighbors, having family get-togethers, and family road trips. Subconsciously, all that time spent around my family and friends shaped my view of marriage and what I envisioned my husband and marriage would be like. I viewed the husbands as the providers and the wives as their helpers, loving each other and working in unity to build a home and support each other's dreams.

Because of my background and the ideas I had about family, I always viewed extended family as an important part of anyone's life, a part that constantly motivates you and celebrates your wins.

We lived the middle-class American life, in a middle-class American neighborhood. Baseball games, family barbeques, and picnics in the park were what we all did on the weekends. My father was one of the first black foremen in one of the steel plants in Chicago; my mother raised all seven of us and went back to work once I became of school age. From what I saw, most of our neighbors lived the same way we did. For a long time, as far as I knew, that was the reality for everybody, but real life began when I joined the military.

I had no idea that so many people outside of my bubble were raised in families with so many different family dynamics, some good, some great, some rich, some poor, some complicated, some painful, some abusive, and some that just didn't even know their family at all. I suddenly started to understand the privilege I had once I began to see the world from a different perspective. Although my parents did a lot of community service for different organizations throughout Gary, I was never really a part of it. That was the main reason why when I had children of my own; I ensured they participated in the community service activities I was involved in. I did not want them to be as unaware as I was about their blessings when I was a child. I discovered that I loved being involved with community service and giving back, which increased my desire to want to do more.

My life has had a lot of ups and downs. My journey has led me to this point, where I am writing this book. There have been a lot of joyful times, as well as devastating times. My life has been filled with adventures, loneliness, rough patches, fun times, and even times when I was at the brink of suicide. Through it all, I always knew that God loved me and was with me wherever I went. After both of my parents passed, I deeply appreciated that they left me with a great moral foundation to stand on. In my youth, I always felt that growing up a "Johnson Girl" had too many rules until I left home; and met people who grew up without that love and structure.

CHAPTER 2

WE'RE NOT IN KANSAS ANYMORE TOTO!!

As I went off to basic training, leaving everybody I knew and loved behind, it was a surreal moment getting on my first plane ride to Ft. Jackson, South Carolina. Having two military parents did not prepare me for what I was about to face. Coming off that plane in Columbia, SC, I had Drill Sergeants in my face, screaming at me to grab my bags and get in line; it was a whole different and confusing planet that I had landed on. These guys looked human, but they were screaming at me like banshees; my brain and body shut down in protection mode. That day, I questioned every decision I ever made in my short eighteen years of living, and I was furious at my parents and oldest sister for not warning me about the nightmare I was having. At that very point, I was convinced that was the worst day of my life… little did I know.

Coming from a Christian middle-class American lifestyle into the military lifestyle was a major eye-opener for me. It was like people from all walks of life coming into one melting pot called basic training; there was absolutely nothing basic about this. We were expected to come together to form a united team, even though we were different in so many ways; I did not see how that was possible.

There were soldiers from New York, California, North Dakota and a plethora of other cities, states, and countries. Some came from the roughest ghettos I knew of, like Cabrini–Green. There were soldiers who were given the option of going to prison or joining the Army. We even had soldiers that had never really seen black people before, except on TV. But, somehow, with all those attitudes and temperaments the Drill Sergeants had to deal with on a regular basis, we eventually came together as One Team, One Fight, and we did it without anyone killing each other. Never would I have expected that most of those roughnecks, big city slickers, country bumpkins, and dirty south soldiers would be some of the greatest battle buddies ever, that I'd keep in touch with throughout my twenty-four years in the military.

The comradery you find in the military supersedes anything else you could ever imagine; you have people from literally completely separate lives coming together to be responsible for one another's lives; it really is a great show of humanity. It is truly a band of brothers and sisters who are bonded through hardships, shared pains, and explorations that most civilians would never know or understand; strangers who become family.

As the United States started getting into more and more wars, conflicts, or missions around the world, the bonds we shared only grew even deeper. Some might imagine that the Army has no time to make bonds and ties, but it is the complete opposite. I can say that it is where the tightest bonds can be made; you see other soldiers go through the worst of times and the best of times, and what makes these bonds is the fact that you share these experiences; you know exactly what the other man or woman is going through, and you emerge together, as One Team, One Fight.

One thing that my exposure in the military taught me is that "common sense" is really not a general thing; it is relative to one's cultural background and experiences. I also discovered that moral and family values are relative to your cultural and life experiences as well. The moral and family value system I grew up with was not part of a nationally syndicated value system, and this really made dating in the military hard for me. Many times, I wondered if the men I encountered were actually raised by women. And if so, did they know the son they raised acted this way. I wondered how those men would have reacted if someone else treated their mothers the same way they tried to treat me.

My mom gave birth to me at forty-three, so my parents were older than those of my peers, which made me naive fresh meat, but mentally older than my years, as I traveled throughout my early military career. I oftentimes felt like I was metaphorically playing dodge ball or being chased around cars as I yelled "quit playin" to avoid men and all their games. Some of my girlfriends and I often laughed about the military being the "Men Mega Mall." It was a rocky road at times, but I quickly learned to toughen up before I got consumed; although, not without some bumps and bruises along the way.

The military back then was much different than it is now. There were so many men in the military that were of the opinion that women should not be allowed to serve our country. So not only as a woman, did you have to deal with the uncertainties of serving your country and being away from home in a male dominated environment, you also had to maneuver through chauvinistic mindsets, especially the ones that were your superiors, and they never failed to remind you that they didn't believe you belonged there.

There are many laws and regulations in place now that prevent most of the discriminatory acts. Before, they were not in place or enforced. Although you can't regulate a male chauvinistic and narcissistic mindset, you can regulate the actions and language it produces.

As I looked back over my career and the military in general, I realized that the military within itself has to operate from a narcissistic point of view. As you are promoted in rank and leadership positions, you have to be able to compartmentalize more to not lead with emotion or empathy. The safety of our country and so many other countries rest solely on the ability of our leaders to make clear, concise, emotionless decisions and some decisions that lack empathy. Also, the rise in rank and getting into positions of power for some people who have a personality disorder is the absolute supreme high. They have a captive audience of people they command who feed their fragile egos. Can you imagine the charge it must give them walking into their office in the morning and having everyone address them with respect merely because of their rank? Whether they are a great leader or not, whether they take care of their people or not, that level of respect by rank has been earned and will be given. It may be easy to develop a grandiose mentality when rank and position allows you to command hundreds of people who speak to you on a daily basis without fail. That is the ultimate fuel for a narcissist, and many of them have to be denied reenlistment or age out of the military because they are aware that that level of fuel only comes with the captured audience of the military environment.

The United States conducts special operations throughout the world, and they have elite teams that carry these operations out. These teams have to be trained to be void of emotions and empathy in order to carry out the missions as effectively and precisely as they do. When their mission is to kill, steal, and destroy, emotions and empathy are not an option.

Their life and the lives of so many other people depend on their ability to carry out their operations smoothly. However, there are a lot of our great military men and women who carry out those missions and are able to compartmentalize or have great family dynamics that are able to not allow the environment to consume them. Our military, in general, is a haven for narcissism, some branches more than others. Being void of emotion, empathy, and personal connections are necessary for the security and protection of our nation. And all the great men and women who serve our country have to endure this, but it is causing our families, marriages, and interpersonal relationships to suffer tremendously from the effects of personality disorders.

That being said, I myself as a Combat Veteran have PTSD (Post Traumatic Stress Disorder), as well, I am a victim of MST (Military Sexual Trauma) but there is a difference when you are aware of your disorder, you seek help for your disorder, actively work to manage your disorder and triggers and allow for there to be accountability. Most narcissistic people will never seek the help they desperately need, unless it becomes an unbearable problem for them. That would also mean that they would have to allow an accountability system for their actions, which by the pure definition of narcissism would be unlikely. I have met a lot of really great people throughout my military career; people of both genders, and I also met some not so great people. As I matured throughout my military career, I came to be painfully aware, that I wasn't in Kansas anymore.

CHAPTER 3

DID HE REALLY CARE?

"Did he really care?" This is the question that we often ask ourselves when our relationships take an unexpected negative turn. Oftentimes, the answer is not revealed to us until we seek help from counselling. People have different ideologies; caring might mean different things to you and your partner. What the other person considers as a caring act can be completely strange and the exact opposite of what you would call caring. As adults, we are a sum of our childhood and adolescent experiences; the good, the bad, and the ugly.

When we are born, the mind is a tabula rasa; it is what we observe from our surroundings and what we are taught that form us. The main stage of our lives that form who we essentially become are our young years, when we are most teachable. By the time we are around the age of twelve, and we hit puberty, it becomes a harder to learn the fundamentals, and when we hit twenty-five, the brain patterns solidify, and it becomes much harder to change our behaviors. Most children who have been victims of trauma in the home or have been around caregivers who do not know how to love properly will grow up with warped mentalities about love and care for others. This happens because, through their teachable years, they may have lacked unconditional love or have been exposed to the wrong kind of love and care from their caregivers. So what was taught to them in their teachable years may still be considered as caring and love to them now. The bad thing is that most of these adults have a hard time dealing with or admitting the existence of this problem, and statistics show that this happens more with men.

Most times, the traumatic experiences will stunt their emotional growth and the ability to mature into responsible, loving and empathic adults, but it does not hinder their physical appearance.

When these issues remain unresolved, they then carry them into different aspects of their lives; to college (maybe an esteemed university even), into their careers, into their marriages, and they may even have access to public platforms to express their obscured views. The scary thing is that these people go on to become important public contributors; they become teachers, relationship counselors, police officers, judges, ministers, mentors, politicians, and many other professions that interact closely, quickly gain the trust of people and influence the minds and lives of the general public. Some of these professions even require closed-door meetings with unsuspected people often. Most professions do not require the clients to have knowledge about the backstory of the professional they are interacting with, and frankly, most people see the title or degree and assume a full background and mental health check was done. Sometimes some things can be missed or even completely ignored due to their title or religious affiliation. But make absolutely no mistake, their dysfunction and traumatic childhood injuries will manifest in their professional and private lives through conversations and actions. Therefore, when you "hear it," or "see it", it would behoove you not to attempt to "unhear it" or "unsee it". Even when you do not know exactly what it is that feels wrong, accept that you feel something isn't quite right. You need to honestly have some internal dialogue.

Sometimes, the problem is very deep rooted; the parents or caregivers themselves may have gone through the same unresolved trauma as children, causing them to manifest into who they are, until everything comes crashing down on top of them. Many times, these caregivers were young teenagers themselves, so being able to give healthy parental love and care to their children was not an option or even a priority. Many of these teenagers may have to leave their children with whoever they can find to relieve themselves of the responsibility for a while, which may oftentimes leave the children unprotected from predators and molesters. Equally sad, the young parent may get into relationships in which the focus is more on their partner and not the child, leaving the child neglected. People that grow up in these types of settings usually get affected negatively, and they have to make conscious efforts to see love in a different way for them to escape from the mental and emotional cages they have been placed in.

Over the years, I have seen a trend happening that I affectionately refer to as "Parasite Parenting." It is when a male child is raised in such a manner that he is made to feel obligated to never emotionally or financially leave his mother when he becomes an adult. Often, we may simply call them "momma's boys," but in a Parasite Parenting relationship, this is quite different and may be hard to comprehend for some.

However, the ones who have been a victim of such dynamics, understand. When a standard parent-child relationship is not established, the healthy roles and boundaries that were supposed to have been in place from childhood do not exist.

In a Parasite Parenting relationship, the child is taught from a young age that it is his obligation and duty to put his mother above all other relationships. So, his role in life is designed around always pleasing mother, even if that goes against God, his marriage, his other relationships, or himself. While I am not trying to pit men against their mothers in any way, there should be boundaries that both parties can respect and understand. Oftentimes, what can cause this is a very young parent or the absence of a father figure while growing up, so they are taught to take on the role of the mother's missing lover and friend, and they are not raised with the expectation that they will be the head of their own family someday. And because these mothers spend so much time grooming the son, they become an extension of her personality, ideology, and mannerisms instead of the child developing their own personality, ideology and mannerisms. The mother conditions the child to be dependent on her approval. This means as an adult, his daily decision makings in life and relationships are often filtered through his mother. These mothers become territorial, and they have a lack of boundaries, and it eventually becomes a competition between the mother and the spouse. Every relationship that threatens the obligatory duties of the mother/son relationship will eventually be required by the son to be offered up for the mother to dissect and destroy it. This is obviously not healthy for any relationship, and this will usually cause discord in all the relationships the son enters into.

I was at a convention center in Atlanta for a conference quite a few years back when I heard a couple having a heated discussion about something. There was an older woman standing by the man's side listening attentively to what was going on when I suddenly heard the man loudly yell, "Well, you are the one who asked me to marry you" in the crowded hallway. The look of horror and shock on that lady's face was heartbreaking, while the woman who was standing by his side looked like she had just felt a twinge of pride. I later discovered that it was his wife he was speaking to in that manner, and the other woman was his mother. The mother did not look significantly older than the man, so I could only assume she was a really young mother when he was born. One thing was clear from that occurrence; that he had absolutely no reverence for his wife, and he was never taught his role as a husband, partner, or protector.

Ephesian 5:31

"for this reason, a man shall leave his father and his mother and be joined to his wife, and the two shall become one flesh."

I doubt he would appreciate anyone speaking to his mother in that way or maybe that was exactly the type of role model he had growing up. I felt bad for his wife because there was apparently a very toxic dynamic between him, his mother, and his wife.

So, the question "Did he really care?" is relative because some of these men are really just doing the best they were taught how. Your actual question needs to be, "Is this what I want for my life?" Or "Is this truly the life God has for me?" You are reading this book, so I can answer that for you…. "ABSOLUTELY NOT."

Jeremiah 29:11-13

[11] For I know the plans that I have for you,' declares the Lord, 'plans for prosperity and not for disaster, to give you a future and a hope.

[12] Then you will call upon Me and come and pray to Me, and I will listen to you.

[13] And you will seek Me and find Me when you search for Me with all your heart.

CHAPTER 4

WHAT JUST HAPPENED?

O ften, when we finally find that special someone who checks off all the "he could be the one" boxes, and some we didn't even put on the list, we are likely to start planning our happily ever after (or at least probably the next ten years) in anticipation.

As women, we spend countless hours and years getting our education, preparing for our careers, raising children, taking care of our families, giving back to the community, and a host of other tasks we take on consciously and unconsciously. We are taught inherently, that women are supposed to be givers, nurturers, and empaths. As Christians, Jesus teaches us to love our neighbors as ourselves, to forgive our brothers and sisters when we have been wronged seventy times seven, and to not merely look out for our own personal interests but also for the interests of others. And to whatever degree this is true for you, what happens when you realize that your Christian principles and truths are being exploited as weaknesses?

Many times, when we see red flags early on in our relationships, we ignore them because we are in the "getting to know you" stages; and we want our feelings of "this is the one" to be true because we really don't have a lot of time to date. I sometimes refer to this as the "butterfly phase." In this phase, things seem to be going as great as they possibly can; and you still get butterflies in your stomach when you think about him. But this is where you will see and hear most of your red flags. On an intellectual level we all know and understand that people are people, so we all make mistakes. There is no such thing as perfection, so with that understanding, you are ready to be forgiving of his mistakes. When mistakes are made, the adult thing to do is to talk it through, with the end goal of resolving the situation, insuring both parties are heard and validated. But what happens if that mistake was deliberately made to test your resolve and boundaries?

Women's intuition is a great security protection device. God loves you so much that when he formed you, he embedded a top-of-the-line security protection device in you to keep you safe. However, just like any other security protection device you may have in your car or house, it only works when it is activated. Discernment works the exact same way; it is only functional when it is activated. Our desire to be in a relationship can often make us deactivate that alarm system because we don't want to scare off any potential partners. We might sometimes make excuses when we witness actions or hear conversations that vex our spirit or make us feel uncomfortable. We may be inclined to ignore the uneasiness under the pretense "he didn't really mean it" or "he was just joking" however..., "out of the abundance of the heart the mouth speaks" As career women, it's nice to have that special someone you can come home to and focus on, someone who can distract you from the day-to-day stress of your office life, someone who can formulate and lead a great plan and make good decisions for the both of you, as well as someone who matches your drive and business sense to be that amazing power couple you've always dreamt about. However, the same innocent desires you have for a loving, secure, and committed relationship are the same desires that can be used to exploit you for unscrupulous motives and personal gain, especially when you are operating in a professional environment and are financially secure. Not everyone who operates in your environment is financially secure or has financial literacy, just like everyone who goes to church is not saved. Being in an environment (professional or otherwise) does not necessarily mean you have done the proper work to be there, or you have earned your spot; it only means you got there, some people cheat their way to the very top.

We have all met fast-talking people who can talk or lie their way into any and every situation, charming everyone they encounter. Many times when we see it happening, we laugh about it, not taking it seriously and keep right on moving, because it's not happening to us......until it does.

The dictionary describes charm as "a power of pleasing or attracting, as through personality or beauty." A man being charming has nothing to do with how he sees you and everything to do with how you see him, and what he receives or intends to receive from you. Charmers are great manipulators, and they pretend to give you exactly what you want and lead you on. They make you feel great about yourself until you do not give them the validation they want, and then they may use other people to get it or ignore you. However, one cannot run on just charm alone; eventually, their charm will fade out, and just as they found their way into your environment, they will find or work their way out of your environment. Charm has nothing to do with productivity, and their lack of work ethics will prove them to be the imposters they are. Activity and productivity will never produce the same results, but you cannot tell charmers that.

It is imperative that you do not ignore the red flags when you notice them. One mistake is that we give the excuse that people change. Yes, people change, but as an adult, it is not as easy as you think. These red flags have become character traits, and they do not go away easily. If you are still willing to make things work, then the solution is not to live with these character flaws; the solution is to tackle them and make sure changes are made. These traits can only change when the person acknowledges them, and the person actively puts the work in to change them and becomes accountable. Seeking help and being accountable has little to do with being a great wordsmith and everything to do with their actions, so, if you notice that they are all talk, and no action, believe what you see. Again, charming is a character trait that is about how they feel, so it has absolutely nothing to do with how they feel about you.

Red flags may also come in the form of jokes or small white lies. You will find out later, that his lies are not so small, and they definitely are not random. Women love a man with a great sense of humor, and charm often accompanies a man that always has jokes. As long as he can keep you focusing on the jokes and charm, you aren't listening to what is really being said (or not said). Laughter is food for the soul, and it has great health benefits. So do not get me wrong, a man with a great sense of humor is very important as long as it's not used as a disguise for deep rooted dysfunction. If you cannot laugh at yourself, your life, or your circumstance, you are going to have a long, painful, and tedious life. No one wants to spend their life staring at the time clock waiting to die. I just want you to be mindful of some of the places where the red flags are. That being said, in the manipulator's mind, laughter and jokes will be used to distract you from some really deep personal and mental issues. We have already established that "out of the abundance of the heart, the mouth speaks." When they say something that clearly does not sit right with you, they find ways to turn it into a joke. They do this so well that they may make you feel like you are overreacting, so you turn off your internal security alarm to be more accommodating because you do not want to make him uncomfortable. So now, your time with him is all about laughing, joking, and having a good time. And because you turned off your security alarm, you will later discover those comments he makes are actually a glimpse of what is to come. You think you are just enjoying your life, but what you will find out later is that all the intimate information you gave him while you all were having a good time is what is going to get you sucked into his game.

However, if you are always laughing, you do not see the deep scars in the pit of his soul that he has been hiding from childhood.

If you are always laughing, you cannot see that emptiness he carries in his little box of horror.

If you are always laughing, you cannot see that inward rage that pops up when something does not go his way or he feels embarrassed or outshined.

If you are always laughing, you cannot see that you are actually standing on the outside of his circle because he cannot let you in, and you really don't know a whole lot about him.

If you are always laughing, you cannot see that he has a problem with closeness and intimacy.

If you are always laughing, you cannot see that he does not focus on you when you talk.

If you are always laughing, you cannot see that he does not even listen to you.

If you are always laughing, you cannot see that his self-worth and identity are totally tied to all the validation he gets from other people.

If you are always laughing, you cannot see that he cannot hold a conversation with you that is not all about you flattering him to make him feel good.

If you are always laughing, you cannot see that when you try to hold a serious conversation about your future, his shallowness will divert it or turn it into jokes.

If you are always laughing, you cannot see that when you give him your heart, he cannot give you his because his heart is controlled by the disorder.

Narcissists always need to be perceived as high achievers and successful, and they will jump through hoops and put up a façade to make people admire them for their made-up success. Narcissists see others as objects, not as human beings, so everyone in their social sphere is seen as something to use. If you are with a narcissist, you will see that they will not go out of their way for you at all but will hurt themselves trying to impress everybody else around you. They may even be so bold as to tell you stuff like, "I'm glad we're married, so I don't have to impress you," I saw a man at a restaurant let the door fly closed on the woman he was with, to go help another woman who dropped some items on the sidewalk. When they have gone out of their way to impress you (in their mind), and you do not show them how deeply impressed you are, they will quickly turn on you, start spreading lies and rumors about you and will tell people about all the things they have done for you and how ungrateful you are. When in actuality, they have not done anything out of the ordinary. Their grandiose facade makes them overstate their involvement in pretty much everything. Because they lack the understanding of reciprocity, they must receive credit and accolades for every little thing they do. They are two faced pretenders; they pretend to like you when they are actually saying negative and mean things about you behind your back. They have a very great disdain for people who will not succumb to their charm. When you see the hatred in their eyes, you cannot unsee it; it is literally a peek into the black hole in the depth of their soul. Narcissists can only disguise their hatred from passers-by; if you live with them, it becomes very apparent. If you are the partner of a narcissist, they have a stare of hatred that can pierce your soul. Once the narcissist knows you have seen behind their mask and you are no longer affected by their manipulation and attempted brainwashing, you will feel that dead stare whenever they think you are not looking. You will then see their passive-aggressive behavior and their burning need to punish you for not appreciating their greatness.

Narcissists send a lot of mixed messages, and you can never really know what is going on with them. They will do whatever it takes to persuade you to believe that they are somebody they are not. They need you to believe in whatever their public persona is, because in their brokenness they feel people would not believe in or love them if their real self was known. However, the truth is, they do not love their "real" self and this is rooted from the fact that they are ashamed of who they really are. Their real self has been broken for a very long time with no attempt by them to repair it because they have successfully gotten by on charm and jokes (in their minds). If they have not been willing to repair their own brokenness, why would you volunteer to take on such an unrealistic task? That decision only means you have volunteered to be used, ignored, devalued, manipulated, lied to, lied on, and cheated on. If you are always laughing, how do you learn about his integrity and true character?

Proverbs 26: 23-28

23 Like an earthenware vessel overlaid with silver impurities Are burning lips and a wicked heart.

24 One who hates disguises it with his lips, but he harbors deceit in his heart.

25 When he speaks graciously, do not believe him, because there are seven abominations in his heart.

26 Though his hatred covers itself with deception, his wickedness will be revealed in the assembly.

^{27} One who digs a pit will fall into it, and one who rolls a stone, it will come back on him.

^{28} A lying tongue hates those it crushes, and a flattering mouth works ruin.

CHAPTER 5

DON'T ACT LIKE YOU DIDN'T SEE THAT!

Being in love is an amazing feeling when you choose the right partner. On the opposite side, the pain of choosing a broken, narcissistic, or disordered person can cause you years of devastation, pain, and financial ruin. So, it is important that as you encounter your potential partner and seek relationships, you do not deactivate your personal protective system just to please him. Here are some specific traits and attributes you need to look out for when you are seeking or in a relationship;

Shapeshifters: Shapeshifters are people who continuously reinvent themselves (their persona) whenever they enter into a new situation, whether it is a relationship, a job, or even a new city. It is different if the person generally just wants a change; that's fine. But shapeshifters do this so that they can fit in and please whoever they are involved with. The reason why they do this is that they lack an authentic inner self; they feel empty on the inside, so they mimic the good and successful qualities of people around them to feel a level of acceptability. Note that there is absolutely nothing wrong with admiring other people's qualities or wanting to have those qualities, but you have to make sure it is not because you lack their own inner-self.

Their entire personality is the sum of the good and bad people they have met along their life's journey. They will be whoever or whatever they need to be to get you to believe in their persona until they finally hone in on the perfect personality that gets them what they need, which is your admiration and validation. Because they are only able to capture other people's outward personal gestures, features, and mannerisms, they are extremely shallow people. They are like light shows; they are nice to look at when the lights are flashing and dancing, but once you flick the switch off, there's not a whole lot there. No matter how hard they study others, they cannot capture the love, the empathy, the compassion, the connection, the bond, the intimacy, or the wholeness other people may feel, and they become resentful for that reason. These chameleons can be extremely dangerous because their whole purpose as shapeshifters is to operate their deception undetected, and they will destroy the entire structure of an organization with manipulation and triangulation to feel validated. And because they have taken on the best personalities of the local people and ingratiated themselves into the fold with charm, you will be less likely to suspect them of doing anything wrong.

Narcissists: According to the Diagnostic and Statistical Manual of Mental Disorders (DSM-5) a clinically diagnosed narcissists suffers from Narcissistic

Personality Disorder (NPD), which is only diagnosed by a psychiatrist. Most narcissists (even if they strongly have all nine traits) probably will not volunteer to be diagnosed by a psychiatrist. Which is different from your average self-centered, obnoxiously narcissistic person, who really should get a clinical diagnosis. It is said that NPD is a personality disorder in which people have an over-the-top pattern of grandiosity, an obsessive need for excessive attention and adulation, a trail of troubled relationships, addictions to drugs, alcohol, or porn, and a lack of true empathy for others. They do not know how to build true and honest bonds with people, that is why they lack the ability to have intimate relationships with their partners. People with the disorder do not have object constancy, which for them means people are either good or bad in their eyes. Lack of object constancy also may mean in an argument; they cannot separate you from the pain caused by the argument. Life for them is either against me or for me. Lack of object constancy for them may also mean "out of sight, out of mind." It is hard for them to feel an emotional connection to you if they are not with you. They gravitate towards whoever is giving them the most attention without challenging their lies or deceit. I had a man tell me one day jokingly that the people at his job did not believe he was married. This guy had been at that job for well over a year. In his narcissistic altered state, he failed to realize that the problem was not with the co-workers or clients who thought he was single; the problem was with him acting single. His hunt and burning need for attention manifested by him behaving as a "social bumblebee" running around, collecting honey by saying and doing anything to get love and validation from anybody and everybody who was willing to give it to him in the workplace. He did not act or talk like a married man; that is why most people assumed he was single and did not believe him even when he said he was married. Sadly, when his wife was out of his sight, she was also out of his mind, which gave him the freedom to hunt. These people tend to be very disloyal partners because of their black and white thinking, as well as lack of emotional and intimate connections. They also have a very distorted self-image and difficulty regulating their own self-esteem, so they need to constantly be around fawning women who will tell them how good of a man they are, and they will devalue any other people who threaten their space so that they can maintain their sense of superiority. They love to create chaotic drama by spreading vicious rumors and lies about people and triangulating them so they can stand back and watch the commotion. They are often very petty gossipers. Seeing other people in pain brings them great joy; they can be sadists, and they will constantly do things to bring people pain for their enjoyment.

Narcissists target strong, financially successful people who are empathetic and forgiving because they do not possess those qualities themselves. They love the idea of a good chase, plus being with someone successful and attractive makes them look good to their peers. Narcissists lack the ability to take responsibility for themselves or any of their actions. Oftentimes (in their mind), the only reason why they (the narcissist) have the problems they have is because their partner lacked the ability to keep them interested, satisfy their every whim, or their partner suddenly went crazy. They are very skilled at shifting blame and are master wordsmiths.

Love-Bombing: Love bombing is the initial phase of a narcissistic relationship used to provoke all your emotions and memory recall. In the initial stage of the relationship, they show an abundance of love and affection to make you feel like you are getting the real man package. Critics of cults use this phrase with the implication that the word "love" is faked and that the practice is psychological manipulation in order to create a feeling of oneness with a person in a very short time period. During the *love-bombing* phase, the phrase "I love you" comes easy to narcissists and will pretend to slip out because there is an agenda of personal gain. Love-bombing is used only to get something from a specific target and never to give something. In just a short period of time, the love bomber can make you feel like you are their soulmate, and you have never felt like that before about anyone, or maybe that kind of love feels too good to be true. Love-bombing is an intentional act to gain control of your mind, your senses, your love, and trust; their aim is to infiltrate every part of your life. Along with flattery, compliments, gifts, romance, or grand promises of a future life together, they purposefully make memories with all your senses (taste, smell, touch, hearing, and sight) to make you intoxicated with them, and they later use this against you in the devaluation phase. They wear cologne to bed to keep your sense of smell enticed when you are around them, so when they are not around you, you notice. They use their fake form of passion to intoxicate your senses through fake passionate kissing (they can learn that from porn videos) to manipulate your mind and body. They are very touchy-feely in private, keeping your mind and body aware of them, but not so much in public to keep you enticed when they are not around. They promise futures and plans that they have absolutely no intentions of following through on. They will go as far as to get a degree in your career field for the future plans of business or make travel plans with you knowing they have no intention of following through. Once they have your total commitment and trust, they have control of the relationship and will manipulate the relationship to get what they want out of it, leaving you in emotional and financial ruin. Everything they do has an agenda attached to it. They will move into your life and publicly make themselves look to be your provider, superhero, your knight in shining armor or your king, and will often put you in very bad or unsafe situations in order to create that public title or image for themselves. This stage can also be called the *idealization* phase as well. This phase contains a lot of extra work and money for them to maintain their deception, which they have already made plans to collect on later.

Manipulation: This is when they use your intense emotional connection to control your behavior. They may manipulate you with overwhelming loving gestures, moving very quickly in a romantic relationship to lower your guard or make you feel indebted to them for all the attention they are giving you. These manipulators pretend to form an early attraction to you so that you think they are serious with the relationship. In a normal relationship, people tell each other all about their dreams and aspirations, about the future and their career goals or their fears and desires because you expect your partner to love you for who you are and share your feelings. However, manipulators pillow talk with you for a reason... not a season, and definitely not for a lifetime. Manipulators seek out information to play on a person's insecurities, and use them to their advantage. They may purposely make you feel fearful about something, unattractive, fat, or old, to control your interactions with other family, friends, or co-workers. It works well in romantic relationships by making their romantic partner think no one else could ever possibly love them as much as they do. Therefore, the partner should just make the adjustment and work on the relationship they already have. A common move for manipulators is moving the goalposts, constantly shifting the criteria you have to meet in order to satisfy the manipulator, which keeps you off balance, and struggling to keep up with some fraudulent standards they have set for you to meet. They will also change the subject in an argument about their behavior; they may deflect attention from themselves by attacking their partner's previous unrelated action like, "Well, what about when you did... ???" or something just as ridiculous. Manipulators use passive-aggressive behavior as well, to undermine their partner with guilt-tripping, giving backhanded compliments, and jokingly saying mean things in public so people can hear or in private. Passive-aggression is a coward's way of voicing displeasure or anger without directly expressing the emotion and looking bad in front of others. Manipulators love to give their partners the silent treatment as a form of punishment, ignoring their partners and lavishing attention onto another person (usually a woman), to punish them for whatever perceived offense the manipulator felt.

Gaslighting: Gaslighting involves the manipulator causing the manipulated partner to doubt their own understanding of reality by denying that the abusive behavior happened, telling their partner there is something wrong with their memory. Manipulators would constantly lie, deny or deflect what their partner claims, making their partner question their own recollection of events; they would do this until their partner is convinced and sees the manipulators point of view. Even when they are caught (to include, boldly on video), they may adamantly deny the lie, go into a rage to divert attention, or cover it up with many other lies, leaving the partner totally confused about if they actually saw what they thought they saw. Sometimes, they will extend the gaslighting to you secretively in public places to evoke an outburst reaction to it. They make sure people only see your reaction, so they will think to themselves, "How can she treat that good man like that?". Which justifies the manipulator's lies told to all the friends and family; "I don't know what happened, she must be going crazy." They make themselves look like loving innocent victims instead of the deceptive manipulators they really are.

Devaluation: I had a woman tell me that years after she and her husband got married, she was reminiscing through his photos, she discovered in their honeymoon pictures, he had posed her in front of multiple other women in bikinis to take pictures of her. When she asked him why he would do something so horrible, his answer was that he wanted to show his friends all the women that were there. He didn't care that his friends saw how he devalued his brand new wife. The *devaluation* phase by a manipulator starts long before you recognize it or feel it, because it's happening in the background. This phase is a confusing time because you go through a lot of rollercoaster (up and down) times with your emotions due to the manipulator's on and off interest in you. You are still holding on to the great memories of the *love-bombing* phase, so you are working through your rough patch to get back to what you thought was true love with your soulmate. Now, your manipulator seems to continuously be on the phone laughing with women (that he says are just friends), despite your objections, or whispering in the phone when he gets to certain points of the conversation, or even completely going into another room to talk on the phone. He may even go as far as telling you how a meeting went where he had all the women in the room cracking up, or all the women he had laughing in the elevator at a different meeting or closing the door on you while he tries to catch a falling object for another woman at the restaurant, or he suddenly has a meeting at 8 pm.

Despite every conversation to talk about the problems end up in denial and unresolved confrontation. You wait in denial, thinking that your relationship will get back on track. Because of the love-bombing phase, you feel that the strong bond that you had can withstand the tribulations; you think you just need to give him more space, or you need to just spend some time working on yourself or fix your own insecurities, not knowing that the love has always been fake. They make you feel like you are the problem, and you need to be more supportive.... Wrong!!!! The narcissistic relationship cycle occurs because they cannot truly bond with people, and therefore, once they get past the love-bombing phase, they get bored and lose all interest in the relationship. It has nothing to do with you; it never did; despite all the lies he spreads to his admirers and friends about you.

Triangulation: Triangulation is another disturbing behavior, and it results in a lot of negative energy and chaos instead of harmony or unity. Manipulators usually display this behavior subtly, so it might be hard to recognize it. Often, victims do not notice their mind is negatively being impacted and that they have become more involved in a lot of negative energy. It could easily become a negative environment of gossiping, being compared to other women, hearing your partner bad-mouthing you to other people, and feeling envious, which can result in you being isolated from your support system and, as a result, becoming more dependent on the manipulator.

Triangulation is a manipulation strategy in which one person does not communicate directly with another person but rather introduces a third person for communication to the second person, thereby forming a triangle. They will inform their partners how a third party, such as a mutual friend or a co-worker, has been flirting with them or asked them to come fix something at their house to cause jealousy and insecurities in their partner. Third-party people that act on behalf of the manipulator are called *flying monkeys*. Sadly, flying monkeys choose to believe the lies and fake persona the manipulator created because they are actually being manipulated by him as well. Anyone can become a flying monkey; it could be naive people who just cannot see what is happening, people that are temporarily fooled because they can't suspect someone is lying and manipulating in such a brutal way, or other toxic people who love the attention, have no boundaries and seem to love messy gossip and drama too. For the most part, triangulation is used to create rivalry or negative thoughts between two people. A narcissist uses it to control the narrative of communication and pushing opinions and beliefs of their victims onto other people. The purpose often is to create doubts and negative feelings in order to eventually isolate a victim from their family, friends or other support systems and make the victim more dependent on them.

Future Faking: Future faking is when a partner lies or promises something you desire about your possible future in order to get what they want now. They give you something to look forward to and make you attached to them. It is actually one of the forms of manipulation that keep you hooked in by making the kinds of future promises they know you want to hear, so they distort reality to get what they want. Future faking preys on your hopes, dreams, and aspirations in order to fabricate lies of a possible future so that they can string you along for an immediate purpose. These promises are definitely going to be broken because the manipulator had no intention of acting on these promises when he made them. Future fakers will reassure you about the income potential they have one day if you would just trust in them, or they can often coax a partner into leaving a high-paying job to be with them or moving to another state to "make the relationship work". They may tell you things like wanting to have a family with you someday, and wanting to get married to you someday, or buying a house with you someday. One of the main things that keep people stuck in a manipulative relationship is financial dependency. Once that manipulator renders you financially dependent on him, he will be able to get far more mental and emotional control. Ultimately, the manipulator will take very little action if any, towards keeping his promises. Instead, they will keep making empty promises or using other forms of coercive control, or passive and active abuse, until you find yourself in such a negative mental and financial state that it is just easier to go along with whatever the manipulator wants.

Uncontrollable Lairs: The "If you aren't lying, you aren't trying" mentality. Some people have been lying to protect all their dark secrets and dirt for so long that it is the only thing that regulates them and their fragmented sense of self. It is understandable that for most of us when we are faced with a dilemma, given enough reason, we will probably violate our own sense of integrity and lie. We quickly calculate the cost of that lie to decide if it is worth the hassle or not. For disordered manipulators and the many layers of childhood trauma and secrets they carry, the lies are a normal part of their life because they do not see the lie as a lie; they see it as protecting their truth, no matter how altered it may be. So, if the lie insults your sense of intelligence, that is a personal problem for you to get over because the protection of their fragile altered truth is what is most important. Their entire life is designed around adamantly guarding the buried lies and secrets they carry, which means they can never let down their guard to allow anyone in, not even you. However, any partner that is with them will unknowingly be expected to guard and carry the weighted unknown secrets and lies they carry as well (with no questions asked). Sadly, the type of people that create this kind of life cannot have loving, intimate, strong, compassionate relationships because they destroy them with weighted down lies, secrets, deceit, and manipulations. They appear to be normal people on the outside; seeming to have tons of friends, being the go-to guy when people need help; they appear to be normal, average fun loving people, but not one person they associate with knows the whole story about them, only fragmented pieces of their life story. There will be major gaps in their told stories, and lots of inconsistencies in their lives in general, but when questioned they will definitely fill in some of those gaps with a great inconsistent lie. Manipulators experience a great deal of pleasure from knowing they were skilled in getting you to believe their lies, because they lack normal human emotions. They are emotionally empty and are often like bored children, they lack empathy for others, and they do not feel shame or remorse about their lies. They will look you straight in the eye and lie effortlessly and guilt-free, even when confronted with a barrage of questions and evidence of the previous lies. If you have ever been the victim of a manipulator's character assassination tactics, then you may know the full extent of the effects their lies causes. Targeting a person's character with malicious lies and false innuendos is the ultimate "going for the jugular" technique, often used out of revenge, for the purpose of winning family and friends' sympathy and loyalty.

Projection: Projection is the denial of subconscious thoughts or ideologies by a narcissist's ego. Inevitably, the Shapeshifter cannot keep up the facade he mastered in the love-bombing stage because they quickly lose interest after you're hooked, and by this time, he is bored of you. Their defense mechanism condemns you by projecting their own internal feelings of worthlessness, shame, guilt, self-hatred, rejection, insecure, inadequate, and confusion onto you. So eventually, after the love-bomb/devalue cycle happens, the partner is usually shocked when the manipulating partner projects his childhood trauma and emotional pains onto them. They can mess with your mind to the point that you really question your own sanity. Narcissistic people have no real self-awareness to speak of because their worth is totally dependent on what value other people place on their lives. That is why they will do anything and everything with anybody and everybody for validation and may claim that the reason they run around looking for love is that the partner does not give them the validation they need. They cannot recognize their own deficiencies and are unable to allow themselves to be accountable for their actions, but will instead cast all the blame for any of their failures and lack on other people; because the truth is their kryptonite.

CHAPTER 6

WHO'S AT YOUR TABLE?

The people you allow to sit at your table will either make you or break you mentally, emotionally, and financially. Do not allow just anybody to pull up a chair at your table; make sure they are suitable to be in your life. Be adamant not to allow gossipy, backbiting, deceitful people who are full of envy, malice, and strife to take a seat at your table. If you find people love to bring you gossip, take a deeper look at yourself as to why. They may bring it to you because you entertain it. Be wary of people who seem to spend more time glorifying their college degrees than they do, glorifying

God's ultimate decrees. Be vigilant to surround yourself with people who are kind, faithful, noteworthy, of good integrity, trustworthy, capable, useful, and accountable. Set your table for Kings and Queens! And surround yourself with Excellence!

The phrase, "Happy wife happy life," seems to be getting some traction from some men who apparently do not understand what the phrase means and seem to be misguided in their thinking on it. They may even tell you that the phrase is not biblically sound, but the truth is, the phrase is very accurate, and the principle of that phrase absolutely is biblically sound. The issue may come from people that were raised in broken homes without creditable male caregivers to teach them their roles in a marriage and home. A happy wife has nothing to do with material possessions or giving gifts like some people think these days. A happy wife has everything to do with a husband (provider) cultivating an environment where there is security, integrity, love, trust, validation, communication, nourishment, protection, and consistency. God's word specifically told you;

Genesis 2:15

Then the LORD God took the man and put him in the Garden of Eden to cultivate it and tend it (that's the home and everything that pertains to that home that God gave him) and

Ephesians 5:31

For this reason, a man shall leave his father and his mother and be joined to his wife, and the two shall become one flesh (reread chapter 3).

Then God told man in

Mark 12:30

And you shall love the Lord your God with all your heart, and with all your soul, and with all your mind, and with all your strength.'

Mark 12:31

The second is this: "You shall love your neighbor as yourself." There is no other commandment greater than these.

Ephesians 5:25

Husbands, love your wives, just as Christ loved the church and gave himself up for her.

Ephesians 5:28

In this same way, husbands ought to love their wives as their own bodies. He who loves his wife loves himself.

When a man nourishes, tills, cultivates, and pulls the weeds from his own land, the land is productive and fruitful (happy). If a man did not see an example of his father loving, cultivating and problem solving in their home as a child and then refuses to acknowledge or accept the fact that he never had that crucial mentoring, he cannot work to actively address that lack he has as adult or husband. Therefore, they may be led to believe that gifts are what make a wife happy, just like the gifts they gave their mother for birthdays and holidays made her feel happy. The bigger issue is a man who does not actively understand the difference between the relationship he has with his mother and the matrimonial unity relationship he is supposed to have with his wife. This is a whole different problem that was discussed in chapters 3 and 4. It is imperative that our society teaches our young men how to be faithful cultivators of the land God gives them so they can be great leaders in their own homes and in society, and not just in persona.

There is no verse in the Bible that specifically and exactly tells men to love their children or a wife to love her husband, but God's word *to love your neighbor as yourself* encompasses it all. Biblical principles should never be used to justify a person's lack or to validate their personal agenda. It is imperative that as believers we unify the body of Christ instead of dividing it. The narcissistic mindset divides and triangulates in order to conquer. God is not the author of confusion. God is the author of *love, hope and peace.*

As more and more children who were raised in dysfunctional environments become college-educated professionals and enter into the workforce or become entrepreneurs and business owners, it has gotten almost impossible to distinguish the true personality disordered men from the arrogant ones. It can be challenging to clearly identify personality disordered people because their entire life has been devoted to living covertly behind a mask, which allows them to get extremely close to unsuspecting people. Oftentimes, you do not realize that they are emulating normal people's societal attributes until you get to know the Charmer up close, on a much deeper level, then you will eventually begin to see, as you interact with them, that they live multiple parallel lives, that don't make sense and don't connect with each other. Although charm and a great sense of humor can be extremely important in a relationship, it is more important to know what is behind the charm and jokes. If you want to know if the charm and jokes are tied to a hidden agenda, watch what happens when you tell them "no" about something they really want or challenge their ideology on a specific topic and watch their reaction. An arrogant person will probably blow you off, whereas, with a disordered person, you may see his anger quickly rise and lower when he thinks about what he has to lose if he's overt, but then, you'll probably see the passive aggression later in retaliation for that incident. Understand, the red flags you see at the beginning of your relationship will not get better later; they get worse.

In the Bible, 1 Samuel describes when, Samuel tried to explain to the Elders of Israel, who were demanding that he find them a King to rule their nation, that they did not understand the function of a king. The Elders refused to listen when Samuel tried to explain to them that their demand for a king was not going to end well. They wanted a King because the other nations had a King. They never took the time to find out what the people of those other nations thought about having a

King. Oftentimes, we go into situations knowing what we think we know or feeling what we think we feel, without paying attention to all the facts.

The Israelites Demand a King (1 Samuel 8:11-20)

11 And he said, "This will be the practice of the king who will reign over you: he will take your sons and put them in his chariots for himself and among his horsemen, and they will run before his chariots.

12 He will appoint for himself commanders of thousands and commanders of fifties, and some to do his plowing and to gather in his harvest, and to make his weapons of war and equipment for his chariots.

13 He will also take your daughters and use them as perfumers, cooks, and bakers.

14 He will take the best of your fields, your vineyards, and your olive groves, and give them to his servants.

¹⁵ And he will take a tenth of your seed and your vineyards and give it to his high officials and his servants.

¹⁶ He will also take your male servants and your female servants, and your best young men, and your donkeys, and use them for his work.

¹⁷ He will take a tenth of your flocks, and you yourselves will become his servants.

¹⁸ Then you will cry out on that day because of your king whom you have chosen for yourselves, but the Lord will not answer you on that day."

¹⁹ Yet the people refused to listen to the voice of Samuel, and they said, "No, but there shall be a king over us,

²⁰ so that we also may be like all the nations, and our king may judge us and go out before us and fight our battles."

As professional women, we may focus a lot of time on our relationship with God, careers, family and lifestyle. So not many things outside of those activities fit into the twenty-four hours we are given daily. Finding a King who we believe is like-minded and is willing to pursue us relentlessly can be flattering. But a man with ill intentions can destroy your life and finances. Narcissists, due to their deep need for love and validation, cannot be faithful or honest in a relationship. They will share distorted pieces of secrets from your relationship with anybody that will listen to them. They love drama, so gossip is their go-to activity, gaining attention with other women by telling them lies about you gets them the attention they want. You will find them on their phones, talking or texting in secret, what seems like twenty hours a day, with multiple women, to get their validation high and so they can feel better about that poison that festers in their soul. They will marry professional high- earning women because it makes them look good to their family, friends, and the public, but they will constantly cheat with other women they would never marry just to validate their existence. Usually, by the time you have figured out that they are cheating on you, they would have actually cheated multiple times before that. Normally, when a person is cheating, they wrestle with some emotional pain or guilt, which gives them away. Because narcissists are empty emotionally, they do not feel guilty for cheating, it actually satisfies their need for validation, which means there is no emotional conflict that gives them away. They get bored easily, which is their justification for being serial cheaters. They breathe admiration and need extreme levels of validation continuously, and one person would never be able to fill that void. Unfortunately, it takes new relationships to get the level of admiration they continuously need, so once they get close enough to a person and the narcissists mask slips off and his deceitful behavior is accidently exposed, he will leave that supply and get a new one. Narcissists love to find people who are in despair to cheat with. If you are going through something, they will be there to act like your knight in shining armor. They will do everything humanly possible to get in your good graces to show you they will be there for you. When you are in despair it is much easier for narcissists to test your boundaries to find out how much abuse and punishment you can take without leaving them, despite their deep fear of abandonment. In God you trust; all others are suspect.

CHAPTER 7

Lord, I Thank You For...
My Protection / My Direction
/ My Correction

My Protection – The fact that you are reading this book is evident that you have been protected and brought through the fire. Protection does not mean you will not face pain, despair, heartache, or discomfort, it means that in spite of it all, you will rise, you will survive. Protection is that voice in your subconscious that says "You probably shouldn't go there; go here instead" or, a scenario where you made a left turn at a corner when you actually were supposed to make a right turn but decided to just go ahead and get to the highway on that route instead of turning around. Later you find out that if you would have made that right turn like normal, you would have been part of a disastrous situation. Protection, many times is invisible; it is keeping you from the harm intended as well as keeping you from the harm unseen. The pains we acknowledge makes us wiser. The things we survive makes us stronger. The things we endure gives us stamina. The hurdles we jump over give us agility. The mountains we climb give us peace. Protection is not meant to keep you from experiencing your life, it is meant to "keep you" as you move through your experiences in life. A safety net that is placed 20 feet from the ground does not stop all the fussing, bad thoughts, pains, and fears that happen to you on that 80 foot drop down to that net. The fact that the net caught you 20 feet from hitting the ground was your protection. You will experience your fears, and you will go through trials and tribulations, but in the end, God will be the safety net that catches you just before you hit the ground. The experiences that we go through in our lives, whether good or bad, are the things that make us what we are, and they make us wiser and more conscious of how to live our lives. God would be robbing us if he did not allow us to live our lives and go through our experiences. But even as we go through life, God never gives us more than we can handle; if he sees that what is coming is too much for us to handle, then he keeps us from those dangers.

Psalm 17: 7 - 8

[7] Show Your wonderful faithfulness, Savior of those who take refuge at Your right hand   From those who rise up against them.

[8]. Keep me as the apple of the eye; Hide me in the shadow of Your wings

God will always be there to protect us, no matter the bad things that we do and the mistakes that we make in life; God loves us eternally, and he will always be our protection.

My Direction – Many times, the things we go through in life are not for us; they are for the people we are scheduled to encounter down the road. Because the pains we acknowledge make us wiser, the things we survive make us stronger, the things we endure give us stamina, the hurdles we jump over give us agility, and the mountains we climb give us peace. It is during those times when we find our direction. Rather than allowing your pain from that flawed relationship to dictate your path, use that pain as fuel and allow it to propel your rise to the highest of heights. When you are going through trials and tribulations, there is no need to panic or give up because you know that it is only temporary and all of that is preparing you for the future. When we face hardships we survive, we grow when we learn from them, and they make us stronger. Life is a cycle, and people always have patterns, so there are bound to be repetitions and similar situations. So, whatever knowledge or wisdom you gain now will make you smarter and stronger at a later time in your life; no experience is wasted. The experiences we have in life are meant to prepare us for the future; they are meant to make us better people for those that we are going to meet in the future, so we must take every life experience as a learning tool, whether it is good or bad. God will always light your path and show you the way. If the things happening around you ever get too overwhelming, you can always look to Him for help and guidance.

My Correction – I used to work for a media company in the early 2000s, and whenever you were in any kind of incident, you had to complete an incident report and other documents. One document, in particular, would truly upset me every time I had to even touch it. This document required you to identify what part you played in the incident and what you could have personally done to change the outcome of that incident. So, if someone rear ended me in a car accident, I had to complete that ridiculous form. If someone spilled a chemical or something hazardous, I had to complete that ridiculous form. If I did something I unknowingly was not supposed to do, I had to complete that ridiculous form. My first response on that document the first couple of times was, "If I hadn't come to work today, I wouldn't have been involved." The HR lady would politely send me back to my desk to write a better response. So, I would have to take that long walk, two buildings over, to get back to my desk, fill the document out to their satisfaction, and then walk back to deliver it to her. After the second time of taking no responsibility for any of it and having to make that long walk back across the parking lot to fill out that document to their satisfaction, I realized that I just had better dig deep the first time, so I would make only one trip. After a few years on that job, I realized that I automatically started to troubleshoot and reroute or anticipate issues I saw coming to avoid having to complete that document. I hated that document not just with "a" passion, but with about four or five passions; however, what I did not realize is that it was teaching me to take responsibility for my surroundings. I could not necessarily change a bad situation that was about to occur, but I could have changed the impact it made or the level of my involvement in it. That was a huge lesson learned that I've applied to my life since. I discovered it to be a very powerful character-building tool in responsibility and ownership that had a great impact on my life and career as I further matured. Taking responsibility for your actions and your environment is very important because it shows the growth in your emotional maturity, and it shows your resilience to be a better and stronger version of yourself. I suggest you begin journaling ways you could've avoided certain situations. Not blaming your situation does not mean that you need to blame yourself. Putting the focus on the abuser is a way of living in the past; abandon the past and move towards the future. What needs to be the focus is finding a solution to the problem you are facing; that is the way forward.

CHAPTER 8

WHY ME?

After reading this far into the book and you have seen all these qualities of a narcissist behavior, I'm sure you must be confused about why you are a target and why you have been chosen. You probably have so many questions. And if this has happened more than once, I'm sure you must think you have bad luck with men. The problem is not with you; you just happen to be filled with all the great qualities they lack and envy. Narcissists do not go for just anybody; they usually target certain characters in people. This means that if you have fallen victim to the games of a narcissist, then you fit the description. Generally, empathic people attract narcissists; they use your empathic nature to their advantage, and they try to manipulate you.

When I mention that narcissists are manipulators, and they like to gain control over people, the first thing that comes to your head is that they probably prey on the weak. On the contrary, narcissists do not actually go for weak people that can be easily manipulated. They go for people who are talented and strong-willed.

Narcissists like to feel good about themselves, so they would want the best possible target. They usually want a challenge so that they will have a greater sense of achievement; they will find it more entertaining when they take down someone that they know is a hard catch.

Narcissists like to feel like the biggest people in the room, and they want others to be envious of them. So they want the flashiest car, the biggest house, and of course, they want everyone's eyes to be on their partner. They will always go for people who reflect well on them; they want everyone to have eyes on them and want what they have. From the outside, the relationship might look perfect, but that is only what the narcissist wants you to see. The truth is that when they are in private, they are abusive to their partners.

Their whole agenda is about control. They want to have full control over the life and decisions of their partners, and they will go to any lengths possible to get that control. For that reason, they don't have other couples as friends, which allows the narcissist to be on a relationship island with their victim. The reciprocity relationship normal couples have would highlight the narcissistic actions and ideology of the narcissist. It is not easy to be in a relationship with a narcissist; one minute, everything is fine, and the next minute, things quickly go downhill.

As I said before, the red flags only get worse as the relationship progresses. As much as you might think that things can change, and he can become a better person, you must be careful, because narcissist cause major damage and are deliberate about it. So if you stay you must do so with extreme caution so that you do not get tangled in their deeper downward spiral of devaluation, depression, lies and deceit. And you must know that if you embark on this very difficult and emotionally draining journey, you must be mentally prepared.

People who have strong family and social relationships and professional careers are prime targets for narcissists. If the person's career has some sort of public attention attached to it, even better for him; he wants a part of it. Their aim is to take control of and completely destroy everything that you have built. The sickening and bizarre thing about all this is that they do it as a form of entertainment or sport, something to get their juices flowing and keep them excited.

Even people who are physically fit are targets. Most men are attracted to fit females and would want to have her; this is an obvious reason for narcissists to want the person. Wanting a fit partner isn't really because he is attracted to the person's body type. He just wants to be able to convey to every guy who might want her that he already has her and he has full control over her.

I will let you know just how bizarre this can become. Narcissists are very judgmental. They sometimes look for people who are strong in their faith, and they make it their sole aim to prove to the person that they can make them go against their beliefs. When a Christian starts to deviate from their beliefs because of the "love" they have for the narcissist, who is really an imposter, he begins to gain control. The narcissist slowly starts to assume the position in the relationship that God occupied until he becomes what she worships and looks up to. It is all a very slow poison that spreads through your life without you even realizing it, until it is too late.

Narcissists like to feel all-powerful and invincible, and they want to feel good about themselves. They will achieve this by associating with people who will make them feel good about themselves, or they will get a sick feeling of satisfaction from taking successful people down.

Narcissists are usually attracted to this type of people;

1. People who are considered impressive in any way. It is just not about how they look; it encompasses the things they are involved in, their careers, their hobbies, their talents, or special skills. Once you are good at something and you excel at it, they would want to tear that thing down. It is even worse if you are good at something, and you are recognized by the public for that thing. When you are getting public recognition, and you notice someone trying to get close to you just because of that thing you are good at, you need to be very watchful.

2. People who love to compliment and show their love to their partners. Narcissists love when their ego is stroked and would like to target a partner that will tell them what a great person they are and reassure them how much they love them and would go above and beyond for them.

3. Anyone who will make them look good in public. Narcissists like to be envied by everyone. So they would carefully sift through options until they find someone that they know most people want, and they would attempt to get that person so that they can show off to everyone.

4. Narcissists are not looking for partners; they are looking for someone that they can rule over. Some people are generally just easygoing, and they do not like conflict, so they tend to stay quiet, even when they know they are being manipulated or cheated. These types of people

are also prime targets for narcissists. They want someone who will not challenge their authority and will submit to them totally. They do not want someone who is ready to fight them to the last; they would rather their partner remains completely submissive.

Narcissists usually have quite unrealistic expectations of their partners, and they also have unstable object constancy, and this often leads them to become unhappy in their relationships when that initial spark is gone, and their partner starts to show their more human and flawed side.

Some narcissists have low self-esteem issues, so they go for people with specific traits that are admirable, and they try to destroy them. There are several types of narcissists, and the ones that do this are called closet narcissists. But in the case of an exhibitionist and toxic narcissists, they generally just enjoy destroying others.

To a narcissist, a successful relationship is one in which they have complete control over the relationship and their partner. Their joy comes from watching the lives of their victims fall apart and get destroyed; it is like an achievement to them. They destroy people's lives with no remorse; they are complete monsters.

I urge you to keep your head up. It may seem like your choice in men may be warped, but I tell you now that you were picked because you are doing well in one area or the other. You are a queen, and you deserve more than what you are going through, and you will definitely have it. It takes courage to heal and move forward; it takes courage to drag yourself out of that pit he has put you in, but you can do it, and God has got your back, so you will come out victorious, with a crown on your head.

CHAPTER 9

THE HEALING

Every stage of our lives comes in phases. We sometimes do not notice it because we are not paying attention. But if you look closely enough, you would know, per time, what phase you are in.

When we make mistakes, for us to get back on track, we need to let ourselves experience these different phases.

When you have been a victim of a narcissist's lies and deception, you cannot just jump straight back to your old life. There are different phases you will need to pass through in order for you to heal completely and to avoid you carrying around unnecessary baggage. You need to be informed about the different phases so that you would be deliberate about your healing process. When you do not fully recover from being in a relationship with a narcissist, you are likely to fall victim again or carry a negative vibe into the next relationship, even though the person turns out to be a good partner.

Here are the phases you need to go through in order for you to get back to one hundred percent.

Shock & Denial: "It can't be. He can't possibly be a narcissist. Things were going so well. Maybe he's just going through something, a rough patch, probably. I think I should try harder; maybe I'm not trying hard enough. I'm sure he loves me deep down. Things will definitely get better."

Even when presented with undeniable evidence, most people will still deny the fact that their partner is a narcissist. And I really don't blame them. I mean, they have probably been together for a while, and they feel like they know their partner well enough. No one likes being made a fool of, so they probably won't want to believe that they were taken advantage of. Narcissists show a lot of affection during the love-bombing phase, so this is usually what the victims hold on to as "better times" in the relationship. I understand that it is a hard pill to swallow, and leaving the relationship is even harder, considering the time and effort that you put into it. But you need to open your eyes to the truth. The denial phase will definitely come; it is completely normal. The purpose of this is not to help you skip the phase; it is to help you get through it. Having an understanding of what you are going through will help you get out of the denial phase.

Pain & Guilt: With time, you will get out of the denial phase, and you will finally see your partner for who he truly is. The next thing that is likely to happen is overwhelming guilt and pain. You may start to feel foolish for falling for his tricks. You will feel very upset about the amount of energy that you have put into making the relationship work. You will probably reminisce on all the times you bent over backward for him, and this will make you very angry.

You may not only feel anger towards him; you might probably feel angry at yourself as well. "How could I have missed those red flags? How could I have been so naive and ignorant? I did so much to please him. I wasted so much emotion and time on him, and he never really cared about me. All I did was see the good in him; I gave him the benefit of the doubt. I feel guilty that I allowed that to happen." The thoughts will just keep rolling in, and you will be filled with anger. While this phase is normal, you need to be very careful. It is easy to get sucked into this phase and remain there. It can make you become a bitter person, and you will take the anger out on other innocent people. If you are not careful in this phase, you can become the very person that put you in the situation you are in.

Subdued Anger & Bargaining: "I have been manipulated, mislead, and seduced. But maybe, just maybe, if I put in a little more effort, they will change. At least, I know what is going on; I can be careful. If I give up just a little more, he may start to love me the way I deserve to be loved."

These manipulators seed themselves deep in your life that they make you act silly and make stupid decisions. You may find yourself slipping back into the relationship, hoping they would change. Keep in mind that these people do not make any changes except there is something in it for them or if they reach a crisis point. You are likely to waste more emotions and time on this journey, so it is best to avoid it. They will find a way to turn things around and make it about them. They may even find a way to make themselves look like the victim.

Depression, Reflection & Loneliness: "After all I have been through, what is the point. I will probably never find the right person. The next person will probably do the same thing. I feel empty; no one can want me now. I can't trust people anymore."

This is a phase that I would advise you not to go through alone. At this point, you feel like damaged goods, but remember you are a queen, and you deserve love. Keep your head up and work hard to correct those negative thoughts you have about yourself.

The Upward Turn: "I think I can make it. There are people who have stood by me through the whole process, and I'm sure they love me. Not everyone is bad; I was just exaggerating. There is someone out there for me because I am worthy of love, and I will surround myself with people who truly care about me."

When you reach this stage, it means that you have come to terms with reality, and you are starting to attain inner peace. At this point, you will start to consider getting back in the game, and you will start trusting more. You start to feel better and look to the future when you come to terms with the fact that not everyone is like him. Evaluate your other relationships and compare them with the one you just got out of so that you do not go through the same process again. Remove everyone who you find to be out of place or negative, but of course, you will need to have further discussions about the whole matter with them.

Reconstruction & Working Through: "I can take the risk of relating again; I have to be able to let go. I take responsibility, but I cannot let him get the best of me."

Accept that you are in no way responsible for the way they turned out. Accept your mistakes, but do not wallow in blame or self-pity. You are not at fault, but you have to evaluate yourself and find out why you were willing to put up with his crap and fix the loopholes.

Acceptance & Hope: "I made a mistake; I am only human. I have not let the situation ruin me; I have only learned from it. I will polish up on my communication and social awareness skills so that I will not be a victim anymore."

Be vigilant and protective of yourself. Know your desires and needs, and do not let anyone use them against you.

It is a tedious and long journey, but it is one that you can make. You need to be strong and courageous. You have it in you.

Now that you understand that you were selected by design, because of all those great qualities you possess like your personal strength, your classiness, your empathetic heart, your attractiveness, your career status, and your financial status. Narcissists have a different moral value system than the rest of the people as to why they seek out certain partners. They attach more importance to the physical attractiveness, public appearance and financial status of a trophy partner, rather than that partner being a good person or a suitable life partner, they need your social and financial status and validation, and they are less interested in your heart.

It's important to spend time journaling your relationship experiences from the very first relationship to present ones. This would include your relationship with both parents and everyone since then. It's important to log your behavioral patterns, because you can't fix a behavior you can't identify.

1 Corinthians 15:58

58 Therefore, my beloved brothers and sisters, be firm, immovable, always excelling in the work of the Lord, knowing that your labor is not in vain in the Lord

NOTES

CPSIA information can be obtained
at www.ICGtesting.com
Printed in the USA
LVHW080041170622
721504LV00023B/361

9 780578 893778